THE GREATER TRUTH

by

RONALD F. VOWLES

Harmony PRESS LTD

Your pathway to God lies within,
Through the beauty of nature
And all that moves and has its being,
Reaching forever upwards
To that eternal light
Of Hope, Truth and Love.
This is God.
Evelyn Vowles

First published in Great Britain 1987
by Harmony Press Ltd. Reading

ISBN 0 946899 03 7

Set in Bembo by JH Graphics Ltd., Reading

Made and printed in Great Britain by Cox and Wyman Ltd., Reading

Contents

Introduction

Through the ages man has been searching for the meaning of life and the truth of his own existence. This search, due to man's own folly and lack of understanding, has been responsible for the growth of many religious orders, rituals, creeds and sects, all claiming what can only be loosely termed the truth based upon faith and belief without knowledge of the truth. The truth as defined by the practising Spiritualist is that the power of GOD can be experienced through the five senses, including the proof of the continuity of life received by the Spiritual senses.

The power which is God, is within all. This truth is often given to us by Spiritualist mediums, the intermediaries between the Spirit World and the material world, those gifted persons who have developed to the state of being a pure channel for Spirit.

For some time now I have known that there is a far greater truth than just saying – 'I know', and proving the continuity of life. Though proof of life after death is the first step for many on the Supreme Path, and a message given to the bereaved from a loved one in Spirit is of prime importance. This advanced Spiritual practice that I have called the greater truth is open to all and lies within each of us. Once you know what the Ancients called the Secret of Life, the Sound of Silence, the audible life stream, and what in the Bible is called the Word, you can surrender yourself by going within and having your own experience completely without fear whether you are aged 8 years or 80 years. The writer is a trance medium, and can say that entering the deep silence within, quietening the mind and coming under the guidance of the soul is not a trance state and does not lead to one, although it does lead to a natural development of the gifts. It is the true contact with the Power that contains the truth, the wisdom, the knowledge, and God's love. It is the Master Intelligence and the realisation that the power – the audible life stream is God – the Word, and as one follows the practice of entering within and surrendering oneself, a little knowledge and truth is released which will become available to the conscious mind in the form of inspired thought. As one's level of understanding develops so the greater knowledge within the power is perceived illumined in colour. It is felt, heard, smelt, tasted, and is a richness of God's love available to all. With continuity of the practice one will become a truly efficient channel for the Spirit. 'Man know thyself' and your Spiritual gifts will develop naturally.

The practice for this development is explained fully, and I have also included extracts from the Ancient Sanskrit Scriptures including 'The Gita' which was written circa 820 BC. The importance behind the introduction of this translation is that we can prove that what they did then we can still do now!

The key that opens the door must be a meditative practice, but once you begin to enter the silence then meditation as we know it ceases as we progress inward with the sound Current. Again, this is fully explained in the chapter relating to the audible life force.

The power is also fully explained as is the Primal

substance which in Sanskrit is called Akash – that time, the infinity, that was before all man's knowledge of creation. An opening to the understanding of the Akashic Records, and the descent of the Soul, is also given here.

I conclude the introduction with an explanation that some of the knowledge I have written about was obtained by research into the Ancient Scriptures. The greater knowledge and higher Spiritual teachings were given during several trance sittings by one who we have come to know as our Spiritual Teacher, Tye Lee.

Ronald F. Vowles

CHAPTER 1

Before Creation

The following quotation was taken from the Ancient Sanskrit Scriptures circa 900 BC. It is repeated in The Vedas, The Upanishads and The Gita, and in common with these Scriptures it is written as God speaking in the first person.

'I am, I am in all there is. I am not this and I am not that, before the Scriptures I am and after all the Scriptures I will be, before creation I am and all creation I am, nothing was created that I am not and all creation is in me, from the lowest to the highest.'

The quotation in the Bible stated, 'In the beginning was the Word and the Word was with God and the Word is God. All things were made by Him, and without Him was not anything made that was made.'

From these quotations we arrive at the point where we say God created all. All Universes, and all life, nothing has its being that was not created by God – the Great Divine Power. It is within the Power that we find the answer, the truth, and the greater understanding that the Power is God.

The period of time before creation has been defined by a Sanskrit word, 'AKASH', which loosely means primal substance. This is only part truth as no primary substance can be greater than the Power. It was the Great Divine Power that created the Primary Substance, the Spirit body that became the cloak of the soul. Neither can the Power be described as an Archytype – the original from which all copies are made. The power remains the same, it is infinite.

It is the infinite life force, the Sound Current, the audible life stream, the sound in the silence, it is within all, what the ancients called the Potent Sound, the Sacred Sound.

All the Scriptures both ancient and modern make reference to the light. Spirit teachers have referred to God as the Great White Light and the Great Divine Light. Silver Birch used the term Great White Spirit, which has greater purity and intensity as one draws nearer to the source of the light.

The Great Power which is pure light is infused with all the colours as seen within the rainbow, and it is a scientific fact that when all these colours are fused together as one they produce pure light. These are the healing colours, each colour moving within its own vibration or light frequency, with temperatures ranging from the heat of the infra red to the coolness of the ultra violet, and all contained within the power. Our spiritual teacher has said, 'The Great Divine Power contains all knowledge, all truth, all wisdom, and is the Master Intelligence, the all knowing, the great love, God's love, and the realisation that the Great Power is God.

All this can be proved by following the Spiritual Practice as related later in the book. At this point we are only interested in the greater truth relative to the Power before creation. The realisation that the Power is God, and the truth that there is only one power, gives us further proof that the power we know and use now whether for clairvoyance, clairaudience, clairsentience, trance states, physical phenomena, or healing (including absent healing) and the power we manifest daily, is the same power and was the same power before creation.

We now have a greater understanding of the power with the knowledge that it can be seen, heard, felt, smelt in fragrance and tasted, and in our innermost thoughts we can visualise the Great Power before Creation, pulsating and vibrating, surging ever forwards. As Jesus said,

'The wind listeth and bloweth and you can hear the sound thereof and you know not from whence it comes or goes', moving through the time which has been defined as 'AKASH'. Which of course leads us into the chapter on an opening to the understanding of the 'AKASHIC RECORDS', and the reason for Creation.

CHAPTER 2

Understanding the Akashic Records

To come to an understanding of the Greatness it is sometimes easier to make reference to a connected secondary that has a direct bearing on the primary. In our case the reference is our own thoughts. Thoughts are live energy forces, often described as living things. We have all experienced at some time the power of deep positive thinking, the force of the thought willing some event or achievement to take place. The deep thought that comes from within, the heart felt wish for the well being of another, the cry for help when in distress that comes from the innerself, that which constitutes true prayer being transmitted within the power and radiating outwards.

We also attune ourselves by going within, into the silence, strengthening the link between the Soul Power and the Divine Power as when sending out thoughts for Absent Healing. The

Power is the same, and entering the silence, connecting with the Audible Life Stream is the way of transmitting all true and pure thought.

Thoughts travelling within the power are analogous to the transmitting of radio waves through the ether, each wave travelling and vibrating at its own frequency, each chain containing its own magnetic impulses of information. This is a realistic comparison of thought waves within the power, each chain of thought containing its own magnetic impulses of information. This has been proved by the equipment used by brain specialists, and also by that piece of electronic equipment known as the 'Lie Detector'.

The deep pure sincere thoughts of love, truth and compassion are thoughts that register and travel within the power, but I am sorry to say that fierce savage evil thoughts have the same energy force and will also travel within the power. Likewise the forces of anger, jealousy, and hate are also moved within the power. Our deepest feelings are similarly expressed.

The magnetic impulses of information within each thought chain are recorded within the magnetic frequency field of the Power. The intensity of the pure light of the power and the colours contained within move at their own vibrations or frequency, and have their own magnetic field. The power, the Great Divine

Power is God, and this further knowledge gives us the proof and the truth that God is the all knowing, and the understanding of how we pick up or sense the thought vibrations radiating from others.

Frivolous and petty thoughts have no strength or energy force and are swept away in the base power of the etheric.

We can now see how God, the Great White light, the Master intelligence, containing all truth, all knowledge, and all love and wisdom, recorded the Divine plan, the Divine purposes affecting all creation. Coupled with Chapter 1 this gives us the opening knowledge to a greater understanding of what has been defined as the Akashic Records. We are able to see how the epic of our lives, good and bad, is recorded, and how when after passing through the Veil we can judge ourselves and our present incarnation from the recorded truth. It is also the truth underlying the statement that our friends, helpers, and loved ones in spirit are only a thought away. Your thought vibrations are received by them through the power.

The Greater Truth of the sincere prayer from within is received by God the all knowing, being recorded within the same Divine Power. In return we receive his Grace and Blessings, the inspired thought, and knowledge of the Divine Purposes for creation.

We accept that everything in being must conform to God's natural law. It must also be accepted that the Master Intelligence, the Great Divine Power, must conform to that same natural law of creation as recorded in the Divine Plan, The Akashic Records.

CHAPTER 3

The Reason for Creation

It may be said that God needed no reason for creating all the Divine Purposes, but as there is a reason and a purpose to all life, the Supreme Architect following the natural law he created, can be no exception.

A study of our own lives will give us a better understanding of the Divine Creator and the reason for Creation.

The Divine Power flows through all, and as we know, the Power contains all Knowledge, Truth, Wisdom and Love, and is the Master Intelligence. It therefore follows that the Soul energy, the audible life force that flows through us, must also contain the Knowledge, Truth, Wisdom and Love. (To strengthen the link with the Divine Power we need to follow the Spiritual Practices as written later in this Book.) In our daily lives we all display some of the knowledge and love we have acquired by going within the Silence. Those developed souls who have built the power within, will radiate this power of love to all as they pass through life. We have all met such people at some time or other. Those who leave us feeling radiant and uplifted.

The mother needs the child to show her love, the mother and father need their marriage union to express their feelings of love to each other. All of us need to have someone we can love. The most hardened criminal has a spark of love that needs expression.

Whether we express ourselves in art, work, music, or caring for others, we need that feeling of satisfaction of a job well done, from which we experience happiness and pleasure. All of us need these experiences, the greatest being shown in kindness, the love given with kindness to others, and the love received when others are kind to us, this is truly God's love. If there is no means for expression then there is no fulfilment.

In the giving of love, advice, material help and guidance to those in need we strengthen the power with our own creative love, whereby the Great Divine Power is enriched by all that we do in his Service. Service to God is the true coin of the Spirit, and that performed by the individual enriches the whole. The individual being in and part of the Whole. The Whole being within the individual.

We are now able to begin to understand that the reason for creation was for the manifestation of God's Great Love enabling the power to express itself, first in the formation of the Divine Plan, and then in the execution of the Plan. The Great Divine Power needed expression for greater fulfilment, and the creation of all universes and all life enhanced that Great Love.

CHAPTER 4

The Birth and Descent of the Soul

The previous chapter has brought us to the final part of the beginning of the search for the greater truth.

God the Great Divine Power created the primary substance, that which is called the Spirit, that which vibrates on a higher frequency and cannot normally be detected in the material life by the physical senses.

The highly refined Spirit was the first of all creation, and is the lighter finer Spirit which is the first protective body of the soul. The Soul is God and in the formation or birth of a new Soul, a minute part of the Divine Power is encased within its first protective cloak which we call the Spirit body. The soul then becomes an individual but still maintains the direct link with the Source of the Divine Power. This is the highest form of creation, the Soul containing all the knowledge, power, wisdom, truth, and the great love, the light and the audible life force, all that is God. The individual Soul at this stage has the freedom to move, think, and act under its own volition.

For ease of understanding; if from the ocean we take a teaspoonful of water and place it in an eggcup, then all the properties of the ocean are contained in our eggcup of water, without of course the direct link between them. The Soul is God within us, and the direct link to the source of the Great Divine Power, and being the highest form of creation its true home is within the highest plane of all.

This is expressed in the Soul's constant yearning to return to God the Supreme, the binding of the Soul's return to the source of creation, which in our search we call 'Religion'.

In the formation and execution of the Divine Plan, God needed many workers and many thousands of Souls were created. These Souls did not become incarnate Souls, but workers within the Divine Plan, who later became the guardians, the Shepherds of Souls, and the Divine teachers. The ones who teach the truth and give direction to the incarnate Spirits upon their return from the density and struggle of life on the earth plane. It must be understood that when the Spirit body returns, that unless there has been some Spiritual development within that individual, the soul is still swamped under the control of the Spirit mental body which is very much influenced by the material world which it has just left.

To understand the Descent of the Soul we must follow the path of those who will eventually incarnate. The actual descent can in no way be related to the physical. It is in fact a descent from the highest level of Super Consciousness, through to the lowest level of Super Consciousness, although this lowest level is still higher than the level of mind consciousness. It is when we go within, into the inner silence, that we are in fact linking with the lower level of Super Consciousness.

Once we know how to enter into the deeper silence we are taking the first step on the Supreme Path, and those who have spiritually developed to this level of understanding will experience the inspired thought vibrations communicated within the power, thereby having their own experiences which will give proof of the Greater Truth, (as explained in the following chapter).

In its approach to the material life, the descent of the Soul is protected by different Spirit bodies each one being denser and heavier than the last, the finer Spirit being within the higher plane of Super Consciousness and the denser heavier spirit body within the lower level of the Super Consciousness. Each Spirit body moves within its own Sphere, the lowest being the etherial sphere, and the Spirit body here referred to as the etheric body. It is the Etheric Spiritual body which is closer to and is an integral part of the physical and material. All in being has its own etheric counterpart.

It is easier understood by describing the frequency of the vibrations of the primary substance – the Spirit. At the highest level we have the extreme high frequency of the vibrations producing the higher refined Spirit, and as we approach the material level the frequency of the vibrations becomes much slower. This explains why the medium must raise the frequency rate of their vibrations within to a higher level in order to obtain communication with the Spirit world. It is the etheric Spirit form that is seen sometimes by the medium.

It was the further slowing down of the frequency rate of the vibrations that formed the first particles of our planet; first the atoms and the molecules, which formed matter, followed by a continuous process of evolution.

The first souls created by God for work on the earth plane were protected by several layers of the Spirit as they passed through the spheres of lower vibrations, the protective Spirit bodies being given the name of the sphere or plane through which they travelled.

It was the etheric Spirit body that was the first form of life on the earth plane, though not in a form that we would recognise today. Then, as the frequency rate of the vibrations of the etheric decreased to a lower rate, the outer layer took a form of matter relative to the material state of the earth at that time. After many different stages of evolution over a period of hundred of thousands of years, we arrived at the precept of man's development as we know it.

In the beginning many life forms were created, all within the Great Divine Power, but there was only one that had the power of the Soul. This was the etheric Spiritual form that evolved to man's state of being, all within the structure of the highest form of creation.

Those of you who have a knowledge of biogenesis and the variation of protoplasm will understand how through evolution over many thousands of years the physical would evolve to a state of self reproduction amongst the species. It was then that the Spirit and the Soul had to incarnate, and for the purpose of life and growth this takes place at the time of conception. The whole process being controlled by the frequency rate of the vibrations both high and low in accordance with the Divine Plan following God's natural law. The Great Universes were created following the same natural law within the Divine Plan.

Scientists have correctly defined the magnetic field force which holds the universes in their individual settings. They have correctly defined the bombardment of positive ions from the sun into the ionosphere – the electric charge that surrounds the earth, they have made a statement in respect of the variance in the frequency rate of the vibrations which make possible the propagation of radio waves through space. This is very good, for it proves what we are saying. They have however, completely ignored that for such things to come about, all following a natural applied law, there must be a Master Intelligence, a Supreme, Natural law operating within the Divine Plan.

The great power within the universes is only a small part of the Great Divine Power we call God. The audible life force, the love, the truth, the wisdom, and the knowledge is all contained within that power and it the greatest power known to man. It is God.

In the next chapter we shall see how it is possible to link with and obtain a command of the power for the greater progress of God's creation, in love, harmony, and peace in accordance with the Divine purposes.

It is the mental Spiritual body that we now refer to as mind consciousness that took control during the evolution of the physical body and the brain. It is the mind consciousness that has the measure of freedom given to us for our peaceful progression on the earth plane, which we call free will. In the beginning it was the soul that had the greater control, the greater inspiration to our thoughts and actions. As we evolved and became more concerned with the physical self and its wants within a material life, the conscious mind slowly took control and eventually passed the point where the Soul and the mind were in harmony.

The Soul became almost completely swamped by the mind, to the time when man forgot and chose to ignore the fact that the Soul ever existed. This state of being remained until circa 1200 BC, when through the constant yearning of the Soul to return home, man seriously started his search for the truth which led to the early Scriptures circa 900 BC. Before 1200 BC man had some knowledge credited to him that there was more than just the physical life as he knew it then, which brought about all sorts of tributes being paid to all sorts of Gods. The beginning of this search accounts for the early statements of spiritual truths that we find in those early Sanskrit Scriptures.

It was not until much later, circa 400 AD that we began to experience the folly of theologians who endeavoured to explain Spiritual Truths in relation to the material and physical life. This folly has continued up to the present time.

The early theologians suffered from a limited intellect, and can be excused for their lack of understanding of the Spiritual truth relating to that period. There can be no excuses for a lack of understanding now. Especially when one follows the Spiritual Practices, having one's own experiences on the Supreme Path to the Greater Truth.

CHAPTER 5

Spiritual Practices Preparation

It has been said that there are as many religions in the world as there are people. This is not the ridiculous statement it may at first appear to be. Especially when we accept that every individual has a soul, and that religion has been defined as the search for the path on which the soul returns to God. We all have our thoughts and notions conceived by the mind, and vague beliefs, concerning God, and the truth of life and death. It is not until we attain some knowledge of the workings of the Great Divine Power and the truth in respect to life that we realise there is a path to God. The Supreme Path that must be the path of all who search for the truth, and higher attainment.

Practical spiritualism starts the search from the beginning with both feet on the floor. The majority of us received religious education either at day school, or at Sunday school. The type of education does not matter, what is important is the fact that you have received some religious knowledge which forms a grounding or basis for the interpretation of the truth. It would appear from general enquiry that most Spiritualists are drawn to Spiritualism when they are ready to search further for the truth. Some of course are born within families who are Spiritualists, others came to Spiritualism through the Spiritualist Church, either through interest or through visiting a medium, sometimes a bereaved person has received a message from a loved one in spirit which will tend to open their interest to the truth, and there are others who have had their interest awakened whilst receiving Spiritual Healing.

Whatever way you are attracted to Spiritualism your search for the truth will go forward with renewed vigour. You may increase your knowledge by reading books, attending lectures, sitting in circle, or taking courses at the Spiritualist College. You will certainly listen to experienced mediums speaking at Church, which is good; you will also receive some guidance. You will probably arrive at a point where you have a sound knowledge of the basis of Spiritualism, and the Seven Principles.

You will meet and talk to other Spiritualists, and make many friends, but, and this is a very big but, if you wish to make further Spiritual progress you can only do this for yourself. No one can do this for you. Others can only give advice, your further development is up to you.

The very first step is to understand yourself. Those words that have been continuously taught through the ages of time. 'Man know thyself', are the finest and truest words of advice that can ever be given to those who are searching for higher Spiritual attainment leading to the natural development of their gifts.

In this book 'Man know thyself', has two specific meanings: Number 1, the outer physical and material self, the ego, the lower consciousness, the senses, and the material mind.

Number 2, the true inner self, the higher spiritual consciousness, the Divine Power, the audible life force, the soul link with God, infinite consciousness.

We now see that we can all write volumes about ourselves, especially in relation to our material lives which must be understood and acknowledged before we attempt to enter within the higher consciousness of the inner self. I use the term 'understood and acknowledged', for it is important to our advancement that we try to clear the decks, so to speak.

Sit down quietly and go back through your life to the early years. Try to mentally form an account of incidents both large and small, good and bad with which you have been involved, those little acts of unkindness performed both in thought and in deed, understand and acknowledge them. Don't raise your ego by trying to blame others, don't push them to one side. They won't go away, all must be understood and acknowledged, so accept your responsibility quietly within. Send out to others you were involved with thoughts of kindness and forgiveness, mentally ask for the forgiveness you need.

What you are doing is actually merging, purifying corrective thoughts into the lower consciousness. You are not putting all your misdemeanours right, but you are now beginning to knock on the doorway to the state of higher consciousness.

You are beginning to make ripples in the Veil of Consciousness, the soul is awakening to the experience of possible changes for the better. Seek and ye shall find. Knock and it will be opened unto you. At this stage you are just beginning to knock, you are in fact preparing yourself mentally to go within into the inner silence, a practice that is a meditative one, and if you have the wrong thoughts or serious problems on your mind these will seriously interfere with your meditation practices as explained in the next chapter.

Before we come to this step we must continue with getting to know ourselves in our daily lives and the effect of the material world around us. We must try to display tolerance and kindness to those around us, and this is not always easy. Living in a material world we have to deal with life in a material way. If you try to go through life being 'holier than thou' there are those who will soon take advantage and walk all over you. The best attitude to adopt is always to do your best with a fair application of common sense.

This chapter has given us the preparation for the start of the Spiritual practices, where we will get to know the inner self, God within, the Divine power within all.

CHAPTER 6

Spiritual Practices
Meditation

'Man Know Thyself, and you will know God.' Before we commence our understanding of the extent and magnitude of this statement, we must first understand the origin and reason for what we know as meditative practices.

Meditation is first the beginning, it is the key that opens the door thus enabling you to enter the inner silence, to quieten the mind and still the body, to merge with the audible life force and to find and link with the true self, the Soul, the Great Divine Light. The earliest knowledge we have of meditative practices is recorded within the Ancient Sanskrit Scriptures, the Bhagavad Gita, though it has been said that the songs of the Vedantas were chanted in a form of meditation before the first letter of the Sanskrit alphabet was formed. We can also follow its reference in the Upanishads and the Buddhist Literature, circa AD 100.

From the Bhagavad Gita, circa 500 BC, in chapter 6, we get the following verses, which most of you who sit for Spiritual Development will instantly recognise.

'God speaks to Arjuna'

1. Day after day, let the seeker practise the harmony of Soul: in a secret place, in deep solitude, master of his mind, hoping for nothing, desiring nothing.
2. Let him find a place that is pure and a seat that is restful, neither too high nor too low, with a skin and a cloth thereon.
3. On that seat let him sit and practise meditation for the purification of the soul: with The life of his body and mind in peace, his Soul in Silence before the One.
4. With upright body, head and neck, which rest still and move not, with inner gaze which is not restless, but rests still between the eyebrows.
5. With Soul in peace, and all fear gone, and strong in the Vow of Holiness, let him rest with mind in harmony, his Soul on me, his God supreme.
6. The seeker who, lord of his mind, ever prays in this harmony of Soul, attains the peace supreme that is in me.

7. Meditation is a harmony. Not for him who eats too much, or for him who eats too little; not for him who sleeps too much or for him who sleeps too little.
8. When the mind of the seeker is in harmony and finds rest in the Spirit within, all restless desires gone, then he is one in God.
9. Then his soul is a lamp whose light is steady, for it burns in a shelter where no winds come.
10. When the mind is resting in the stillness of the prayer of meditation, and by the grace of the Spirit, he sees the Spirit and finds fulfilment.
11. Then the seeker knows the joy of Eternity: a vision seen far beyond what the senses can see. he abides therein and moves not from Truth.
12. And when he sees me in all, and he sees all in me, then I never leave him and he never leaves me.

Meditative practices have been carried on down through the ages and form the basis of most Eastern Religions. Meditation in its purest form is the contemplation of the audible life force, the Sound current, the word, the true conception of the Supreme one.

Meditation was also known and practised in the Western World. Christian Mystics and the early Church Fathers had their own systems of meditation and obtained results which were highly valued by them at the time. They were most jealous of their achievements and tended to keep the practice a close secret.

The Abbot of Mount Athos in the eleventh century gave this account of his methods of meditation as follows.

> When thou art alone in thy cell, shut the door and seat thyself in a corner, raise thy mind above all things vain and transitory, recline thy chin on thy breast, turn thy eyes and thy thoughts toward the middle of thy belly, the region of the navel, and search the place of the heart, the seat of the Soul. At first, all will be dark and comfortless, but if you persevere day and night, you will feel an ineffable joy and no sooner has the soul discovered the place of the heart, then it is encircled in a mystical ethereal light.

Not perhaps the recommended point of concentration, but it does show that they had knowledge of how to go above the lower chakras. It is not within the extent of this book to discuss the religious practices of all Ancient Religions, except to say we have gone back in time as far as those written records permit, and it has been ascertained that the religious thoughts were purer and more simple and the beliefs more rational in the earlier period, than those in later times.

The knowledge of Divine Attributes and Spiritual Practices faded when the masters and teachers passed into Spirit taking their knowledge with them. Their followers were very quickly distracted by the attraction of the material life, and the finer Spiritual Knowledge gave way to creeds, rituals, and dogma, held together by pomp and ceremony, brute force and ignorance, each forming their own religious ethics.

It was this which brought about the downward trend, and a general deterioration in meditative practices. Spiritual practices were carried on mainly by the priests and monks of that period.

Meditation as we know it was not openly practiced until around 1780, sometime after the Renaissance period. It is interesting to note that this revival took place both in the Western and Eastern parts of the world at the same time. The Hindus and the Sikhs fought over their beliefs, the Gurus and the Masters showed themselves openly, and the Buddhists' strength grew in proportion; the Ancient Spiritual practices were once again being taught to their followers.

Meditative practices were only slowly accepted in the Western World being looked upon as barbaric and evil, and something that smacked of the Witchcraft of the Middle Ages. (Depending on the use of the power, they may have been right!)

Meditation today is practised by many people in this country, in many instances by groups for health and relaxation. The Western Buddhists and the Spiritualist movement have been the main exponents in this direction.

The purpose of any meditative practice is a Divine Purpose, leading to a Divine Revelation. Meditation is only the key that opens the first door to the inner self. Whatever the means you adopt for your meditative practice, it is purely a personal one, that which suits you best, remember no-one else can do it for you!

Once you have decided then stick with it. Whether you decide to meditate on various texts, the repetition of Holy or Spiritual names, beautiful flowers, the movement of the breath, or listening to music played at a low level, the end result must be the same, the opening of the door leading to the inner Super Consciousness. It is at this stage that meditation must cease – the repetition, and the music etc, turned off. you will find when arriving at this point the need for silence as you commence to go into the innerself. When you start your meditation have patience. The accent is on practice.

This is only the beginning to what has been referred to as Deep Meditation. I prefer to say contemplation, because it is also at this point that we should be linking with and merging into the Audible Life Force. With meditation we need something to meditate on. When entering into the Silence and Stillness we hear the Audible life stream and contemplate on this sound, as we go further within, so we now refer to contemplation and not meditation.

This sound can only be heard by the inner finer hearing of the Spirit ear. Everyone has the capacity to listen and merge with this sound, the audible life force, you do not need to be a medium to connect with the sound current. This will be fully explained in the next chapter.

Returning to that stage of our meditation where we commence to enter into the inner silence. I state most categorically that you will not become aware of the true self, the super consciousness, until the consciousness of daily life, time and place have been completely lost.

As long as you are aware of time and space, you will not enter into the depths of the inner silence, you will not see the illuminations of the Soul, the true self, God within.

The inner light which is pure light has been referred to as illuminations because we do of course also see the colours that make up pure light. The extent of one's seeing during this stage is a chink of pure light, colours of light, sometimes momentarily, at others waxing and waning, and for a split second pure light tinged with violet that blots out everything, and on rarer occasions a large ball of fire similar to the sun.

Variations of the above are seen intermittently during our practices, each individual's experiences being different according to their spiritual progress. The greatest knowledge is in the inspired thoughts received after each sitting, either at the time of the sitting or during the days to follow. We are all individuals within the Great Divine Power and are all Spiritually at different levels of consciousness.

It is within this third stage that some give up before there is any genuine experience. It must be stressed that the whole process is one of continuous practice, practice and more practice – stilling the physical body, allowing freedom and harmony of the spiritual bodies, going into the silence and quietening the mind, allowing freedom and growth of the Soul.

Many give up through fear of the unknown as they start to enter the real silence within, some are afraid they will not come back. If you are afraid you will not come back, I can assure you, you will not go!

Once you have learnt how to merge into the audible life force, you are under the complete protection of the Great Divine Power and you can surrender yourself into the deeper stillness and silence without fear.

It is in the depths of the third stage that you reach the point where you must surrender yourself, that point where the body and mind are gone, relating only to the outer physical world.

The awareness we experience now is one of our innerself, nothing else exists, the feeling of being wrapped within soft velvet, within the great peace, to receive our own experiences, to see the inner light.

'He who has been there will know what I say'

'Be still and know that I am God'.

In respect of the posture of sitting for one's Spiritual Practices I can do no better than to refer to that taken from the Gita as printed on page 34.

The development is entirely up to you. As with Spiritual healing, we all have the potential within but the development is up to us. Going within, linking into the super consciousness, will also enable you to develop naturally, and will enhance those gifts that may have already developed.

CHAPTER 7

Spiritual Practices
The Audible Life Force

In various parts of this book reference has been made to the audible life force. It is the sound current of the Great Divine Power and is an integral part of the whole Divine Life Force that radiates from the source and permeates within all. It is the very breath of life that can be heard, without it nothing would live, it is God within.

In coming to a closer understanding of the Greater Truth we can prove the existence of the audible life force, and the light within the Divine Power through our own dedication to the Spiritual Practices.

Contemplation on the audible life force for the purpose of going within and entering into the super consciousness is not new. It is a practice that has been carried on by the Eastern Religions and taught by the Masters and Gurus down through the ages, being referred to in the early Ancient Scriptures as the Potent Sound, and the Sacred or Holy Sound. The Hindu masters at the present time are teaching their followers the Spiritual Practice of Contemplation on the sound current. The Masters say that all without exception can reach the highest Spiritual Attainment whilst on the earth plane, having their own experiences to the extent of seeing various levels of the Astral Plane, and being able consciously to remember what they have seen and to whom they have spoken. The main attributes being constant practice. The extent of opening to the super consciousness of the Astral Plane is the fourth stage in our meditation and contemplation.

We must now commence our understanding of the Divine Sound Current and what the inner ear is listening to. The Buddhists call it the thundery silence, or the sound of silence, the Chinese followers of Tao call it the voice of God, the Hindus call it the Surat Shabad Yoga, the Sound Current, order or voice of the Supreme one. The Upanishads call it the Potent Sound, and in the Gita it is called the Sacred Sound of creation. It has also been referred to as the Divine Melody and Celestial Music. In the Bible it is called the 'Word', but we shall refer to it as the audible life force.

The audible life force never stops, it is surging forward all the time, it is moving through all, it moves within us without interruption. We could not live if it were to stop, the life force and the sound is always there, being part of the Great Divine Power which is God. We do not hear the sound when our minds are active and especially when our minds are engaged on material activities. The mind therefore must be subdued and this is the prime reason for our initial meditation.

The Audible Life Force

To describe any sound is impossible, the nearest we can get is either to imitate the sound, or as in this case, to say what it sounds like. The writers of the Ancient Sanskrit Scriptures had the same problem. It is written that when a devotee connects with the super consciousness the first experience he has is to become aware of ten sounds reverberating within him. From the Upanishads of the Rig Veda we get:

'First he will hear the sound of waters resembling the waves of the ocean, the falling of the rain, waterfalls and cataracts. Then at intervals the sound of a vibrating drum. The thundering cloud, the bell and the conch will come.' From the Bhagavad Gita we get the Sacred Sound, – the OM, AUM or HUM, it is produced as a continuous note by uttering the word AUM, without closing the lips to form the M. This is not the highest Spiritual sound heard with the inner ear. The note varies as one progresses higher within the super consciousness.

I will now describe the sound from my own experience. First, the location where the sound is heard, is behind and level with the top of the eyebrows encircling the head level with the top of the ears and heard from within, concentrated at the third eye centre. Once you have connected with this sound current, the audible life force, you can prove its existence by closing off the physical hearing to the outside world and continue to hear the sound from within. Once you have connected with the audible life stream you will never lose it, you will be able to merge with it and contemplate on it at any time. The sound itself is at a comfortable level of hearing though at times it varies in strength.

The first sound I heard was like the hissing of rain falling on the road in the distance, this incidentally is the first sound you connect with every time you sit. The second impression is like waves rolling on to the sea shore, and the sound one gets when putting a large sea shell to the ear and listening to the sea. At varying intervals one will hear a fine ping, and a prolonged note of a delicate bell, and also a sound like music with no definite tune. When you are entering the deeper silence you hear and feel the thundery silence that envelops you like a cloak, as you continue the Sound of the OM comes in over the top something like the soft hum of the pure note of a dynamo. As said before the sound of AUM without forming the M.

The sound recedes becoming quieter as you approach the innermost self which is now your awareness of nothing else but the sound and the super consciousness. I have said that you can contemplate on the audible life force at any time. It is also possible at any time to sit quietly for 10 minutes and concentrate the mind on the seat of the third eye, situated between and level with the top of the eyebrows, and at the same time contemplate on the audible life force without going into the very deep silence. This is a very good exercise for development to the Spiritual practices.

The Spiritual Practice of Contemplating on the audible life force, is one of constant practice. Connecting with and hearing the various sounds will take time, it is all up to you. After connecting with the first basic sound it will still need continuous practice for the greater development, but connecting with the audible life force is your assurance of the Divine Protection as you travel the Supreme Path of the Super Consciousness.

CHAPTER 8

Spiritual Practices Salient Points

The practice of meditating is something you can do anywhere at any time, but it has been proved that the best progress is made when you sit in a quiet place on your own. If you sit with your wife or husband then you must sit in complete harmony with each other.

To meditate is simplicity itself and all are capable of obtaining that inner peace and progressing into the higher consciousness. To help the beginner I have included some of the more salient points as follows:

With a view to exercising some control over the mind to enable man to obtain some peace within himself and relaxation of the physical body, it was found that giving the mind something to focus and concentrate on was allowing the mind to react in a normal, repetitive way. The object being to hold the mind's attention and control the thoughts, thus slowly quietening the mind. The mind can only be subdued by the mind

The mind's attention is focused at the third eye centre and held there, while the thoughts concentrate on the subject of your meditation. (The subject is one of your own choice.) What really matters is the uninterrupted practice of your concentration. Starting with 15 minutes, and building up to one hour daily. This may of course be spread out through the day according to the time available to you.

The third eye is located between and level with the top of the eyebrows. The third eye is known as such because we normally see through the two physical eyes which look outwards and cannot see within, some other perception is required to see within so we call it the third eye centre. There is really no eye at all which you have to find inside. Jesus called it the door of the house, but then there is no door either. Without the veil between the Soul and the mind consciousness being removed you also cannot see inside. We are of course talking of spiritual vision. The terms third eye, or door, are just by way of explanation. The veil is the veil of consciousness.

The opening of the third eye simply means that we start seeing visions as we progress spiritually. When you see the light, the colours and other things this is due to the inner perception of the higher consciousness, it is that we call the third eye.

When you want to remember something or think deeply you automatically concentrate here, because the seat of the Soul and mind is here at the eye centre. The energies of the mind consciousness are scattered throughout the body and are drawn to the eye centre during meditation. Hence we start at the eye centre, we do not start from the lower centre, nor can we start at a higher level. Everything is within the body, and your consciousness is drawn to the third eye centre and then in turn rises higher as you progress. This is why you may experience a numbness or coldness of the limbs, because as you quiet the mind, the body automatically becomes still and relaxed as the energies of consciousness are withdrawn. Ignore this experience as the breathing and circulation will take control of the temperature of the body with continued practice. The breathing should be left to take care of itself remember the subconscious is capable of looking after the body whether you are conscious or not.

Where is the beginning and where is the end? Consciousness does not physically start from the eye centre and physically end at the top of the head. From a lower level of consciousness you go to a higher level of consciousness, and then on into a super consciousness, a continuous process of development.

When you close your physical eyes, you are there where you should be, you are at the eye centre, unless your mind is roaming on other things. When you close your eyes do not try to find a particular spot, do not invert your eyes physically or try to search by moving the eyes because the eyes should in no way be strained. When you close your eyes you are automatically there. Hold the mind's attention focused on the eye centre and concentrate your thoughts on your meditation. When you are able to hold your attention at the eye centre and begin to go within you will commence to slowly hear the sound of the audible life force, this should with practice pull you upward in higher consciousness towards the inner light.

The eye centre is not a physical centre, it is pure spiritual consciousness. You may have heard of the pineal gland and the pituitary gland, but do not try to mix the physical and the spiritual. Forget glands, the body is full of glands that will all decay with the body.

Sometimes we experience different sensations as the body relaxes, and some people attribute all sorts of weird and wonderful happenings to these sensations. Do not worry about any sensations at all. They will pass as you continue with your meditation practice. You must not become conscious of any thing – keep concentrating on your meditation, with the mind focused on the eye centre. Even when you see a flash of light, or colours etc, continue to keep concentrating. If the mind or thoughts stray, bring them back. Keep concentrating. Practise, Practise, Practise. This way you cannot fail to make progress.

Do not start thinking of going within, that will come naturally. For withdrawing the consciousness to the eye centre you may use any method of meditation to concentrate on. But above the eye centre you contemplate on the audible life force as explained. As you go deeper within the silence then the thoughts and meditation will cease and the outside world is left outside, and you will only be aware of the inner self and the faint but clear sound of the audible life force. Contemplating on this inner sound is the path to the super consciousness.

CHAPTER 9

Mind Consciousness and the Trance State

The sense of consciousness runs throughout the entire body, and we are normally conscious of all body sensations from the toes to the top of the head. It is this consciousness that is slowly withdrawn to the third eye centre when we meditate and subdue the mind, being aware as we go within of a numbness of the limbs, and then losing all consciousness of the physical body, and the material world around us. Ultimately we arrive at the state when we are only consciously aware of where we are within ourselves, having lost all consciousness of time and space, with a feeling of being secure and at peace and where we slowly become aware of the faint but clear sound of the audible life force.

We are now at a slightly higher level of consciousness than that experienced within the activities of the physical, mental, and intellectual.

There is only one mind, but there are innumerable levels of consciousness, each level being obtained as a result of one's own personal spiritual attainment.

As the veil of consciousness is lifted, our progress is within the realms of the spirit linking with soul consciousness, the light, the power, and the audible life force, all that which is God.

We have referred to going from a lower level of consciousness to a higher level of consciousness. We have also made reference to a lower and higher level of super consciousness which is just another way of expressing the level of consciousness pertaining to higher regions of the spirit world.

The difficulty is in coming to an understanding of this higher state of consciousness without first experiencing that state. Unless we are consciously aware of a particular state of being then we find it difficult to accept unless we receive proof of its existence from another direction, i.e. a message proving the continuity of life.

We can prove that there are higher states of consciousness through our spiritual practices, but we are unable to prove the extent of the higher levels of super consciousness. Although we accept the fact that they must exist, as with God, the Great Divine Power, we can prove the existence of the power, the light and all it contains, but we are not able to point to the source of that great light of purity, although we do accept that the source exists.

If we examine our own physical consciousness, the lower level we use in our daily lives, we find there are periods we are not conscious of, as when in sound sleep, or under anaesthetic, but we do know that the higher spiritual consciousness does not sleep or become unconscious, because we do remember certain things at various times upon awakening and we also remember experiences received when returning from the deep inner silence.

The states relating to trance, however, are completely different, and for those who may be concerned that surrendering to the inner silence is a state of trance, I will explain the difference.

There are many levels of trance ranging from very light trance through to light, medium trance, that misnomer semi-trance, and deep trance.

Spirit friends and controls have told us that due to the interference experienced these days, ie electronic and motorised equipment etc, the medium has to be put into a very deep state of trance when engaged in any form of physical phenomena.

The states of trance are still within the control

of the mind until we reach that state of deep trance where there is no physical consciousness. The mind, however, is still used by spirit controls.

During the levels of very light, light and medium trance, the consciousness of the mind is awake, aware and knowing, with the mental faculties active. In the semi-trance state which is the last stage before the unconscious state of trance, the mind is consciously aware and often can hear what is being said by the control. It has been said by many experienced mediums that it is within this state of semi-trance that the higher evolved minds of the spirit world find it easier to make contact. The mind is still used by the spirit control when the medium is in the deep unconscious state of trance, and only a small part of the mind is subdued by them to obtain the unconscious state.

In the early stages, states of trance are obtained by self inducement, what might be referred to as a self hypnotic state, but one that is still under control of the mind consciousness. The difference is that during the development of trance the consciousness is not going from the lower level to the higher level of consciousness, but rather the reverse.

Most spiritual mediums are in a light form of trance when they are working. Spiritual healers are also in a similar state of light trance especially when impressed or having the hands moved to a particular area. This is what is commonly referred to as the state of attunement.

It can readily be seen that everything we do is within and under the control of mind consciousness. Spiritually and materially it is within us to take the first step, to play our part in our own development, thereby allowing spirit friends to play their part.

I advise anyone wishing to develop trance to have a spiritual assessment, and I strongly recommend the Arthur Findlay College at Stansted Hall, Stansted Mountfitchet, where you will be told of the depth at which you may be over-shadowed by spirit, and also given some valuable instruction on trance development.

CHAPTER 10

Progressive Thought

In the beginning man sensed the predominating influence of God, being aware of the power, the light, and the sound within all. But due to his low state of intellect he was unable to reason any further than that which was necessary for his survival, being surrounded by all types of wild animal life and various types of vegetation. The prevailing experience within himself at this time was fear.

Fear of the unknown, fear experienced from lack of understanding due to his lack of intelligence, then the fear and panic experienced when strangers came near, and the fear of having his possessions taken from him. The fear he experienced is similar to that experienced by wild animals.

The difference in man is of course the Soul and the Mind Consciousness. The mind consciousness had already taken over at this time and led man to form in groups for his own protection giving him a feeling of security. This in turn led to larger groups, tribes and villages, the essence being survival. There was, however, some social involvement and forms of right and wrong instituted within the tribes. As life evolved man began taking a closer look at his surroundings and became aware that there was something greater than himself that he could not see, hear or touch. His fear grew at this greater experience of the unknown, and he was also very much afraid of the dark. His fear created all sorts of fantasies. The sun, moon, stars and the seasons were looked upon as the greatness and when the sun or the moon became clouded over, their thoughts grew that they were being punished, and this led to offerings and sacrifices being made to those unknown which were considered to be the greater beings of power. This no doubt encouraged the first thoughts of reverence.

Man started his inner experiences with fear, and this fear has remained with him until the present time. As man evolved and became more intelligent so his thought and reasoning power increased, and he soon found that his selected beings of power did not come up to his expectations. Seers of that time had visions that were subjected to many variations of thought, that resulted in many forms of idols and gods, and sacrificial rites being performed. It has been said that since this time over 3,000 different religions have been founded, and we can see how many have stood the test of time.

We must however give some respect to early man in his endeavours and search for what we call the truth. We must not forget that this was all he had and all that he was able to understand. In some respects he may have been better off as there was no-one to brainwash him, as with those who followed in later years.

One of the gods that is worth a mention is one of the early Egyptian gods, 'Anubis' the god of the Necropolis. He was a man with the head of a jackal. His function was to weigh the soul against the weight of the feather of truth, before one could enter into heaven. I wonder how many could have passed that test! Man continued to make progress through the period of Greek gods in the Pantheon, through that time misappropriately named Paganism, up until the early formation of the Aryan races. It was within this period that the seers and mediums of the time received their visions and inspired thoughts, and were no doubt under the control of the Guides. The Old Testament makes reference to the control of 'Yarvie'. Yarvie being a Spirit Guide of that time.

It was these early visions, thoughts and revelations that inspired the songs and verses chanted by the Vedantas and later became the Ancient Scriptures when the Sanskrit alphabet was formed. It is as a result of the beautiful grammar within the Sanskrit Scriptures that they are amenable to translation. These early scriptures formed the basis and teachings of the Eastern Religions, Hinduism maintaining the advanced form of Spiritual Practices to this day. The Old Judaic System with its beliefs in the sacrificial lamb had been handed down from time immemorial. The Epistles formulated by St. Paul, an educated Jew, schooled in Hebrew Law were written much earlier than the Gospels and were based on the Old Judaic System with Jesus now being the Sacrificial Lamb. Paul thus gave the world its first taste of Christian Theology. Jesus' Spiritual mission and teachings underwent the usual corruptions and mis-statements of the theologians, and Jewish followers found their fulfilment in this reconstructed Judaism, historically founded as Christianity.

The pure philosophy of Eastern wisdom became submerged in dogma and rituals. In the Ancient teachings sacrificial deaths had been accepted as a matter of necessity. Now they could justify that Jesus died for the sins of the people!

An attempt has and still is being made to formulate the teachings and songs of the Vedas, the Gita and the Upanishads, into modern language adopted for the requirements of the Western World. Some excellent examples can be obtained from the Penguin Classics, many of the Sanskrit translations coming from Cambridge University, translated by Professor Juan Mascaro, an accepted authority on the Ancient Sanskrit Alphabet.

We can now see that man has always had a need to believe in something that would help him in times of stress and trouble, and in the past the major factor in bringing a religion into being has been timing, to suit man's need at a particular time. A good example is Islam, the Religion of Mohammed the Prophet, bringing the Arab races together when there was need for unity, and at one time covering all of Persia and a third of Europe. Even now, 20 per cent of the World still bow their heads to the Islamic faith. The need for a belief in a Supreme being has been motivated by man's prevailing experience of fear, and a consciousness of thoughts from within himself that he did not understand.

Every religion, caste and creed, with their dogmas and rituals have played their part, however dubious, in the evolution of religious practices and man's Spiritual Progress. The one great thing that has been overlooked and misinterpreted in most of these religions has been the Spiritual Practices.

Love of God, love of one's fellow man, good ethics, being kind in thought and in deed, moral thoughts and conduct, are most excellent when we endeavour to carry them out, but they can only lead to the Supreme Path. It is the dedicated Spiritual Practices that will put you on this Path and Keep you there.

For over 60 percent of the population of the world true Spiritual Progress is almost non-existent. Man lost interest in his search for the truth. The material life, together with Science and Advanced Technology had taken over. The more advanced Eastern Religions were continuing to teach their followers the now established Spiritual Practices of the Masters, the Guru Saints.

In other parts of the world many churches were being closed, and serious seekers of the truth were looking elsewhere. It was then that Spiritualism as we know it today came into its own. Spiritualism was providing the major part of the knowledge of truth which had been ignored in earlier teachings.

Spritualism and Spiritual Practices have been carried on through the ages by mediums, but were now allowed by law to come out of the shadows, and credited as a religion, taking its place in respectability alongside other denominations.

Spiritualism and its Spiritual mediums have given seekers after the truth definite proof of the continuity of life after what we call death, proof of existence of the Spirit body, and the Spirit World, and that in fact there is no death.

It is this knowledge that will eventually destroy the inner prevailing experience of fear that has been within man since the beginning. Once the proof of survival is accepted by all men then man will be able to understand the full meaning of the greater truth and the experiences he can have by dedicating himself to the Spiritual Practices. When this time is reached we shall truly have one religion, and the real meaning of the word – Religion – 'the return of the Soul to God' – will be fully understood.

Spiritualism is playing its part in man's Spiritual progress, and will continue to do so for some time to come, but it is the teaching of the Spiritual Practices that will become the crucial and decisive knowledge in man's future progress, that will allow him to go further within the Super Consciousness, and in time to step out and return at will from those higher spiritual regions in full consciousness.

When you reach the highest plane, the source of the Great Light of Purity and Creation and the last cloak of the soul is laid aside, when you look into the brilliance and see your image reflected in the Great Light of perfection, you will then fully understand, and will truly be able to say 'I AM HE'.